тне
bLue HOUR

WISCONSIN POETRY SERIES

Ronald Wallace, *Series Editor*

the blue HOUR

Jennifer Whitaker

THE UNIVERSITY OF WISCONSIN PRESS

Publication of this volume has been made possible, in part,
through support from the Brittingham Fund.

The University of Wisconsin Press
1930 Monroe Street, 3rd Floor
Madison, Wisconsin 53711-2059
uwpress.wisc.edu

3 Henrietta Street, Covent Garden
London WC2E 8LU, United Kingdom
eurospanbookstore.com

Printed in the United States of America

LIBRARY OF CONGRESS CATALOGING-IN-PUBLICATION DATA

Names: Whitaker, Jennifer, author.
Title: The blue hour / Jennifer Whitaker.
Other titles: Wisconsin poetry series.
Description: Madison, Wisconsin : The University of Wisconsin Press, [2016] |
    ©2016 | Series: Wisconsin poetry series
Identifiers: LCCN 2015036820 | ISBN 9780299308643 (pbk. : alk. paper)
Classification: LCC PS3623.H5626 A6 2016 | DDC 811/.6—dc23 LC record
    available at http://lccn.loc.gov/2015036820

for Tom, daily

Contents

II.

acknowledgments

These poems first appeared (sometimes in a very different form) in the following:

Beloit Poetry Journal: "The Invention of Childhood" and "Habit"

The Boiler Journal: "Throat-Song" and "Home"

Cave Wall: "Story in Which the Daughter Briefly Encounters Providence" (as "Story in Which the Children Briefly Encounter Providence") and "Story That Begins with a Bat Falling Dead"

Connotation Press (A Poetry Congeries): "The Gown" (as "The Gown, on the Occasion of the Daughter's Tenth Birthday"), "The Invitation," and "Collusion"

Drunken Boat: "The Lesson" (as "The Swallow")

Four Way Review: "Something He'd Do" (as "Something He Did")

The Greensboro Review: "Father as Distant Boat" and "Story That Begins and Ends with Burning"

James Dickey Review: "Daughter as Pallid Bat in the Attic" (as "Child as Pallid Bat in the Attic") and "What to Wear to a Father's Funeral"

The Louisville Review: "Daughter as Collection of Words" (as "In the Dictionary of Ballet Terms")

New England Review: "The Look of It"

New Orleans Review: "Father as Barred Owl" and "Father as Map of the World"

Modern Grimmoire: Contemporary Fairytales, Fables and Folklore: "Aubade"

Pembroke Magazine: "Mount Vernon" and "Blue Hour" (as "The Blue Hour")

Radar Poetry: "Mother's Foxes"

Sugar House Review: "Rumpelstiltskin"

Many thanks to the generous staff and editors of the above journals; to the MFA program at the University of North Carolina at Greensboro; to Ron Wallace and the fantastic editors at the University of Wisconsin Press; to the North Carolina Arts Council, Trudy Hale at the Porches, and Joan Houlihan, Martha Rhodes, and the wonderful poets at the Colrain conference for providing time, money, and communities that fostered the completion of many of these poems.

Thank you to all those kind enough to offer instruction, help, and/or the generosity of friendship, encouragement, inspiration, and understanding: Alan Benson, Gerry Canavan, Fred Chappell, Jim Clark, Kim Cuny, Stuart Dischell, Camille Dungy, Michael Gaspeny, Holly Goddard Jones, Alysia Joost, Terry Kennedy, Sara Littlejohn, Jennie Malboeuf, Michael Parker, Jeanie Reynolds, Shana Scudder, Greg Shemkovitz, Mark and Katie Stollery, Laura-Gray Street, Rhett and Jeff Trull, Peter Wohlwend, and Lee Zacharias. Love and gratitude to Lynette Whitaker for her years of support and good faith.

To Rebecca Black and Jaimee Hills, who read and commented on (many) drafts of this book: unending thanks. And to Allison Seay: you can't know.

To Jim Peterson, for first believing in my work, and for mentorship, friendship, and kinship: thanks aren't enough.

To Denise Duhamel, I'd like to express my profound gratitude for believing in this book.

Finally, to Tom and to Huxley: you make all of the hours lovely. You have my whole heart.

тHe bLue HOUR

Last Poem about my father

It was his body carried over the threshold
        on our wedding day; no, *I* carried it—
                skirt hitched up to hip, my necklace of straw,
shouldering his heft like my one true child.

        No, he was light as powder,
                caught in a draft and settled into corners.

If I am a puzzle, the picture
        I kept making was *his*:
                victim, conspirator,
mirror, slut, secret,
        tunnel-to-get-lost-in.

He died, and ten years later
        I left his bedside. In my decaded vigil
                I made a dress of his dying:

skirt scalloped with his swearing, crinoline
        of piss and sweat, his emptied bed
                a sour bow at my breast.

I fell in love, married, but was a bride of sighs
        trapped in a tower of his bones,

pulling the cloak of him around me at night.
        I drank his blood because there was no water.
                He the detail in an art book,

someone's fine shoe filling a frame,
        the whole world a plucked dove and her surrounding light.
                He the gleam of light

on a pearl, the pearl itself, the crooked post pierced
        through my ear's lobe.
                He my hood of improbable red,

my crumb-scattered path,
        my wolf finally thrown in the stove.

How else to say this? I am sorry for bringing him in,
        for making him ours.

I.

the Invention of Childhood

Believe it: Father made the world just for me—
        the sunlight fluttering like ribbons in a pony's mane,

the river a pony I lead through the hills.
        This lullaby he licked clean: the riverbank

peddling hellebore's fat pods, flowers antique and verdigris-hued.
        The fence he painted the dulled color of comfort. Believe it:

he made me this lushness, these extravagant blossoms cut and vased.
        Made me a porcelain tub, mildew-slick,

and called it *river*, the water flushed red,
        clear again. Made me a bird shot through

with light and called it *defiant girl*.
        Bang, he points with forefinger, thumb straight to heaven,

my youth already over, the tiny eye an explosion of red.
        The neck a soft torn cloth. The beak blown to dust.

Something He'd Do

On days cold enough to remind him of home,
my father, whisky-warm, dragged from the shed

the kerosene heater, sending the rangy dogs
to the fence line. The overfilled tank, the choke

of kerosene soaking ragged into the wood floor,
he coaxed the heater to hot blush

with a single match and finally slumped to sleep
next to the trailing hair of its heat, its burning chest,
its hot mouth gagged with rags.

tHe Look of It

Make it December, roughly. Leave her speechless
on the bed in the linen-colored morning light.
Supply the details: air cool as a lizard's back,
blankets thrown to the floor, door swinging wildly
on its hinges from the man's leaving.
Fill the empty spaces with the slap of bedcovers
thrown back, the smell of lime soap,
bruises mapped purple-black across her legs.

Take from her the whirring hush of sleep,
the sweet smell of gas heat in winter,
the clean water rush from the faucet.
Now let her ease out of bed,
soak her gown in the sink. Watch the shadows
of pear trees shake at the window like bodies.

fATHER AS BARRED OWL

How could we not recognize you that spring—
the distinctive, quavering call, face sallow as ash.
Hunting alone after sunset, you must have fed all night.
At first, the forest-wealth of bobwhites and chipmunks thinned,
and in daylight, dense hair and bone littered the ground
under the Virginia pine you loved. By the end of the season,
you caught more than your need in that thin-river kingdom:
in the morning, pale snakes sizzled belly-up on the banks,
small opossums lay frozen, mid-snarl. You lay frozen
while we paced in our house that spring, and the feral kittens
shook under our shed, alive with flies.

Strange Sister

The night is catalogued like a set of animal tracks—
where hands *where* dragged *where where*—
until rain hits the gate like thumbprints,
until floods carry him away
and she crawls out.

She is asked for details,
those facts that slit the cut again:

the marquis sign of the convenience store
across the street that night,

      ATM   HAMS   OYSTERS,

pluck of air against the skin,
swelling-shut eye that narrowed
the world to a blade.

Something dead was close,
a squirrel or rabbit,
so that, too, is added:
sweet smell of decaying things,
that strange sister of things safe,
wet mulch, the wild fistful of orchids
growing nearby—

Story that Begins and Ends with Burning

Help, as usual, arrived too late. In jugs slung across
        the backs of cows, the water sloshed and spit itself out,

the daughter tugging and hustling the animals
        flameward up the hill.

By the time she reached it, the house lay in charring heaps,
        the trees hissing like blown-out wicks. The daughter knew

she should've burnt too
        and spent the soot-stained afternoon

watching herself in a reckoning blaze:
        bound up in the curtains, fingers fretting hot cloth,

holding a melting plastic pail
        twisted like a wrung bird's neck,

chaining herself up in the dim attic
        and oh the savage heat of it all—

But let her rest now. Let her lie down in the ash
        and shut her eyes. Let her always wish the house

back to burning—when the portraits still held
        a familiar flaming hand or eye,

when smoke rose into the air like new blooms,
        when a door, smoldering but whole, was still there to be opened.

tHROUGH tHE VINES

and slips of weeds the man is dragging,
dragging the girl across the beds of trees.
She sings of cows and dishes and spoons,
moons, other glowing bodies of cool and light;
it's as if she made him, and this dragging,
she thinks—she's nursed this fear daily
and now this pulling is real—and he's pulling her hair,
pulling her to her feet.
                                    But he's gone now, released
so she drags herself, each day dragging
to that place in the small wood where he took her,
and she, pulling a blade from her dress,
makes cuts—one for each day of creation,
and one for that long day of rest.

Habit

When I followed him to the river, I narrowed myself
to a needle's point—the morning clear,

the cicadas' swelling hum a comfort.
Lures spread out carnival-bright on newspaper,

those feathers trembling. The day's catch usual:
fish too tiny left on the banks, a snake flayed open to the light.

The field beyond the river: the cattails bending
with the wind, those daffodils' pursed lips.

When rocks bit the backs of my knees,
the haze of insects crowding around us,

my skirt pushed back like a gasp and the water
the water a stagnant slash across the land

I didn't fight. I was older then. I wasn't scared;
I was tired.—Back at home, I brushed my hair,
put on my clean dress.

tHE INVITATION

It arrives complete with castle, horse and rider, papercut-thin,
crackling upright at a touch. It arrives but does not tell

how the cupcakes will be perfect and how I'll cover mine with sprinkles,
slur the icing on my fingers and lick them clean; how I'll watch

the birthday girl's father watch me do this; how there will be an animal
strung from a tree, crepe-paper body flustering at the glancing hits

until her father—one aim—splits the horse's back,
and the evening collapses; that I'll be the last one to go in,

sidetracked petting the dog, when he comes out;
that he'll stand silhouetted by porch light and ask

don't you wanna play a game?; that every other person in the world
is already inside, and so I lift up my dress. I lift my dress

like it's something that will save me, an upside-down parachute
with bow and buttons up the back; the shadows are pants at his feet,

sloughed like a shed skin as the belt's snaked out,
so I lift my dress because in the lifting it won't tear,

lift the dress because that must be the price of all this fun,
the charge exacted; I lift my dress around me like a prayer,

and he recoils—a slap—spitting *nasty girl, you nasty girl* over and over,
an incantation, a protection against me, pulling me inside

where the good children already hide, and the birthday girl,
stumbling in the dark, grasps for something familiar.

tHE LESSON

The heat that summer was a body itself,
your dress a damp cotton skin.

> As he planted the hydrangeas violet and fire-red,
> you found it—cat-ravaged and dim—
> and it rocked in your open palms as you hurried across the yard.

In the backyard's tangle of pine needles,
eyes shut, your narrowed hearing—

> When you asked him to save it, he did, in a way—
> the swift crack of its neck in his hand—
> snap of kindling-burn, chair's back splintering, a switch on the skin—

until his hand slammed
over your mouth, a silver river at your neck—

> and he buried it there, his thumbprint of blood
> on the leaves covering a mouth froze-open,
> a velvet-tunneled throat—

the Birth Premature

opening those tiny eyes you would've seen
       watching you among the others
       in the room where all the early bodies
       like plucked chickens lay
those blackened buzzing things
                    all fester and wretch
bringing the gifts of your birth

happiness and beauty and charm
your face blank and smooth as a sheet on the line
your curls and light eyes and small lips quick to please
your summer dresses

stupid girl
could you not wait to get here
did you not see what gifts would come

Mother as Blossoming Vine

This is how I want to remember you:

your firm hold in the heft of fear,

your pink trumpets waving to me in the wind.

faLse Season

Because it felt all day like spring
I remembered

       the new yellow-green leaves blown down from showers
       him tracking them tiny and bright down the hall

and in his arms a bag full: bracelets with twinkling charms,
the glass-spun ballerina, plush pig and a duck,
the pale horse with a brilliant blue mane,
the glossy covered books,

            those spines unbroken

In the Sick Room

Are you feeling poorly baby
He sits me in his rocking chair in the darkened room
       presses a hot palm to my hot forehead
the world is stuffy and drooping but he holds a pitcher of water
cold as stone in his other hand
relief, *relief*   it's always the same in the dream
he is watching over me in an empty house
keeper of the thing I must have

The morning I watched a swallow hop its slight weight on the wire
      the sky unleashed behind it, the wire
      glinting in the sun like a silver chain pulled taut
I knew to have this was to be forever happy

Are you feeling poorly baby
In the dream his trochaic concern draws him close—
feeling poorly baby—
      he smiles at the wet bird of my tongue licking the pill from his palm
      the cold water some kind of blessing

Then a late-morning game show whispers from downstairs
      the roulette clicking the wild applause
Spin the wheel come on down
      girl please come on down

fatHer as Map of tHe WorLd

You, brittle rawhide sheet, coaxed smooth.

You, stained with careful navy rivers,
margins of principalities and kingdoms.

At first you embraced the local animal, copse of birch,
lemon tree, swamp tangled with snakes.

Then you were rewritten, your sheep-filled fields scratched out—
the wolves now lean and roaming.

Gone the fishes and toads, gone the trees with gasping blooms.

What choice had we but to fill the unknown spaces
with starving beasts, with waters that drown.

father as Ribbon in My Hair

The story of the bird stealing a girl's ribbon is true:
It was summer and the shimmering green of you disappeared
in the beak of a finch as I walked through the field.
We set the cats out to find the bird, and gone
were the cats all days, only to slink back,
fatherless, through the fields at dusk.

Perhaps you're the first thing just-born birds see,
smooth on their egg-cracked floor. Perhaps that's you
the crows keep returning to, snagged on a branch.
They pick and pick at you, snatching bright bits.
Perhaps that's you in all this heat.
Lonely you say into my ear.

Rumpelstiltskin

She suspects a name for him packed with ill vowels—
one that begins with a curling tongue pinned to the palate,
a punch to the gut, plosives and spit and hiss,
the mouth cracking open to a forced smile at the end—
but it is always just out of reach, the taste
of peach in winter, the old river's copper rot
upon waking. The livery of his sin
marks the path she'll follow out:
denim wasted and stained,
belt and buckle threading tightrope-thin,
T-shirt a wrinkled defeat on the floor.
As he labors over some anonymous want,
she worries the augur of another morning:
she'll follow the path to the field,
the wild sway of wheat. The ever-darkening sky.
Her dreams twist and bind.
Waking later, she watches the spider silk
twinkle gold on the sill, with no recall
of the render, the unctuous, nameless pact—

tHe Gown

Start with the anxious declension of the evening,
with his pleasure at seeing my fingertips
touch the fabric, start with the gown's soft folds
as it unfurled like a surrender in his hands.
Start with black silk and lace,
start with the camisole straps thin as picture wire.

Or I could start abstractly—
the improbability of remorse in a room like that,
the air filter's constant hum,
a locked door promising him
the susurration of sheets,
streetlamp sliced to blades, fanning
unnatural light across the floor.

Or start with how
he brushed my hair over my shoulder,
straight-pinning the straps to fit,
how later one of the pins slipped just under the skin
and when I closed my eyes I could see it there,
a tiny light burrowed in my back,
how like the spindle in the book it seemed
as I fell into a fabled sleep,
                    the whorling out of hours—

How did it start? It's too late for beginnings,
unfolding time: the gown was a bouquet of grown-up women,
the smell of Mother sleeping in another room.
It crumpled and stained and later smelled strong of sweat,
was never washed—just boxed back up

to be put back on, bodice hanging concave at my chest.

Wait, begin again: with the woman at the store

creasing pale pink tissue *just so*,

                          his imagined wife floating before her

                          like perfume on the air,

with her question, *a special occasion?*

                          and with his answer: *yes.*

Story in Which the Daughter Waits for the Hunter to Return

The forest was a wall of calls at dawn.
     She lived alone, at first

keeping her hands and teeth scrubbed,
     eating fruits from the failing garden,

shuttering the windows like a good child at night.
     In autumn, the hunter brought her a bit of deer,

left her feasting and fattened. She memorized
     his footsteps' clomp through the fallen leaves.

But then the well water soured, the shutters cracked brittle,
     the walls sagged to soft rot—

her last candle burned down, a lump of wickless wax.
     She watched the grasses tangle up around her,

listened to the branches scrape at the roof
     in the wind. Alone, she grew bright-eyed, hungry.

Alone, a soft fur covered her belly.
     She knew the animal would come:

after all, the desperate attracts its own kind.
     Early in winter, she recognized the pale gold eyes

dipping in the dark like lanterns,
     the hooked claw fiddling the lock.

Do you think that the hunter will save her?
     Spot the sand-gray cloud circling the house?

Nail its hide to the door? The hunter is dead
     and the house a forgotten shadow in the woods.

Daughter as Collection of Words

In the dictionary of ballet terms, there is a violence
you can't imagine. At first, the words fluttered
around Madame like moths, flimsy, ephemeral—

then written out on the chalkboard at the studio's end
       jeté   frappé   tombé   battu
a daily allowance of words
turning over in our mouths like peppermints,
now hard, now sweet.

With their meanings I picked the lock of ballet's secrets:
       to throw   to strike   to fall   beaten
       these words that told me back my story, making it beautiful—

so that I didn't flinch when her cane crashed the downbeat
on the wood floor, swollen and creaking in the heat,
       our spines strung straight as a belt pulled taut,
       the salt striating our legs—

didn't flinch after class in the changing room
       damp as the inside of a lung
as I peeled off my slippers like a rough skin, stripped away
the black leotard and peach tights,
       the other girls' eyes lingering like cool cloths
       on the welts raised on my back.

When I looked up through the clerestories
the night sky spread into a fairy-tale wood
       where I heard myself whispering a new language
       that almost led me home.

Mount Vernon

The evening after I showed my father
a glossy biography of Washington,
we began the building: the model's walls
of wooden dowels, hot glue luminous in the lamplight,
meticulous spread of black paint for the plank shutters,
five coats of red to perfect the sloping roof.
        But that night, the model drying in the corner,
I was kept from sleep by the slight shadows
starting to spot its painted front lawn, the mountains
beginning to swell at the tiny home's edge,
the stranglevines already taking hold.

Story that Begins with a Bat falling Dead

The daughter threading a string through its wing,
        hanging it up in the willow. And there she loved

the bat and decorated all the willow with her dead—
        the moths, drowned in hot wax,

the hummingbirds glittering with garnet throats,
        the clay-black foxes, the wasps and the rats. She felt their eyes

looking after her, their slack mouths whispering
        in the cool night. A slight creaking in the tree meant rain,

a dull rustle meant wind in the field; by sound, she accounted
        for all of her dead. But eventually, the bodies began

to fall, piece by piece, away. Eventually,
        and this is what scared her, the bodies made no sound at all.

BLUe HOUR

The whole world swells
underneath the house;
old newspapers bloat
in their plastic skins,
a black heat damps
like the inside of a mouth.

I quit the whine that sent me here,
I crouch in the bright six o'clock dark
like a cave cricket, in its fear
and ricochet frenzy blind
and springing toward that which frightens,

that which could easily be you—

II.

Snow White as Apology from My Youth

In the absence of predators,
she made one of me:
saw me as threat, as covet.
The white cut of envy
cleaved her mirror's image.

In her image of me, my eyes—black as a crow—
saw only her, my skin pale as the birch tree.
My red lips revealed a mouth of her blood.

I relented. I admit—
I played the part to a tee.
She sent a hunter: dumb man
wooed by my tears, my coos.
True, some would call it murder;
I call it fortitude.
The hollow tin of the train
brought back to her, deadly, me:
I sent the garnet heart
from the man's knotted chest,
and the man's eye
staring back: bright green.

Daughter as Painted Boy

When [Pope Leo X] entered Florence in triumph, he had a young boy painted gold....
The boy died shortly afterwards, poisoned by the gold paint on his skin.

The Medici: Godfathers of the Renaissance

Painted gold sole
to crown, he knew the sun
shone through him.
At the banquet, he spun
the evening to a precious point,
watched the ladies, shuddering ships,
navigate the room. The hand
of His Holiness dripped
like melted wax
to the gushing queue,
lazy smoke from a blown-out taper.
But the music swelled
too loud and the boy grew dizzy
thinking of all the pies stuffed
with birds he'd heard trill *peek-a-boo*,
their music-box chests,
their little glass bones,
the sad trundling bear
chewing its paw to nub in the corner.
The peacock—organs
and entrails removed,
the ribcage cavern
stuffed with others' meats—
whispers to him as it,
plattered, parades by:
boy of gold boy of gold
your day is his to end.

COLLUSION

Daffodils smashed under my bare feet
as I ran to catch you
        tearing from the house

and as you turned to me
        the ornate golds and reds of your necktie, a bird's wing-glint
        in evening's low sun
I saw I'd twinned us with this choice—

the blossoms and the fading light bathing them like flames
the smell of sulfur and the curtains quickening to ash

        the match and the hand that strikes it
                equally would burn

Cinderella as Wish that Comes true

Every day rises like this:
pouch of a fake mother's frown,
sisters fussing the dishwater curls at their necks.
Their demands toll constant;
my dress frays ragged
while they swoon at themselves,
ribbons and silks and voices like bells.

Every night begins with my wish
as I'm gowned in fog on the lawn:
Man in the moon, be a prince—strike a match.
Burn out the stars in their dumb minuet.
Forget the clock; let it drone what it may.
I'll stare until everyone shatters like glass.

Daughter as Sister in Many Layers

Once a grown boy for his time begged the bed
of a sister: the plea believed sincere, only hers
the perfect fit, only hers held lock, held key.

And when did she give in, bachelor's buttons
blue bursts across the field? maybe
the pumpkins' swollen rows? or the wooden ache—

no, no season knows its origin, no season
will claim it. There, in the moment of this story's start,
a light clicks on somewhere: a sunset,

a mother tidying the kitchen, a father
checking the door. The light turns on in sighs:
one, two, three, and ah the cut of her courage,

her tiredness and sleep, her binding up
in layers as in furs: to spook the boy,
to keep the boy at bay, the wool, the cotton,

dresses and sweaters; she'll scald to the touch.
But in its bulk the boy sees only heat,
smells only salt, the succor of his want, her trick

just a game to tease him. Pleased and pleading,
he peels each layer from her and regrets
only: waiting this long to begin.

Story in Which the Daughter Briefly Encounters Providence

After the horn split the air like an axe,
        the hounds' barking a fog in the night,

after the stumbling, sleep-riddled run, she reached
        the balloon in time, its blue and gold fabric

just where it should've been, a luminous skin
        slack on the moor. The sack of apples

survived the trek untorn. The first match burst
        the fuel into flame. Even her small dog,

three days dead and dragged by a bloated paw,
        would make, it occurred to her, a fine roast over the fire.

The balloon filled up like a salvaged lung.
        She could rest now, slumping down to sleep deeply

as she rose through the pinpricked stars,
        with each moment the kingdom shrinking away

to more and more nothing. And now, look out
        ahead of her. The day is just beginning.

Don't you see the jagged blades of light she floats toward?

Rapunzel

Each night in her doorless room
his hand tangles
in her hair—trick lock
of his buttons undone—
and she thinks she'll chop it off, her hair
and his snarled hand,
leave a matted nest on the floor.
By the time they realize
she's gone it will be autumn,
and the leaves will drop
like meat from the bone.
She will have already dreamed
her ladder: light braided
along the floor,
paper chains, a blanket
anchored and thrown.
She will have thrown her rope down
to exactly no one waiting.

mother's foxes

On days when I am sullen, I think of them:
fox of envy, hollow fox with black punched eyes.

Skittering fox skirting the road, fingers-in-the-pie fox,
egg-stealing fox licking thin black lips to red? Pretty little doll-fox.

Fox of bad nerves and pill-fox, Scotch-fox forever coupling
with glass-fox. Fox of the lamb and fox of the knife.

Closer, fox, and I trick you into my arms: whiskers
tasting the air, extravagant tail collaring my neck, your gekkering

echoing through my empty rooms. Fox of mother's thoughts,
I swaddle you in song and whisper into your fearful, laid-back ears:
In what wood did you leave your young. To what hunger.

tHROat - SONG

In his dying he was a bird with a jewel
caught in his throat, struggling and soundless.
Alighting on the bedpost, he cocked his head
at the pinched smell of eggs dyeing
somewhere in their small tins.
His razor beak clicked open-close,
open-close, the choke dumbing him,
panicked feathers falling
to the unmade earth below.

Listen to me, little throat-bird:
those are your stunted eggs,
rank and shocked garish with color.
Listen to me: I am that stone.

Story in Which We Scream at the Daughter to Stop

This is the old story: it was desire that deafened her.
        Unanchored and left to drift,

the daughter crossed the sea, the guideless moon
        pale and sick-green like the sky's old bruise.

The water whipped at her, tongued
        the boat's hull, constantly promised her shatter.

Nearing land, she listened to the dark animals
        of the shores. In the end, she made herself an offering—

cast out of her boat, torn up, picked apart
        by those needle-thin beaks, those snouts.

In her fear she heard the animals
        calling *this way*

come this way you're safe
        rest here you small one

which is how she translated the shrill screams,
        the plaintive hungry yelps, how she saw

the entire kingdom as an imagined father:
        benevolent, willing, able to save her first from himself.

aubade

This isn't how the waking goes: delicate brush of lips,
kiss of sunlight, a single red rose at the breast.
The glossy pages try to spin this lie to gold

but it's the older story she knows is real: land dry
as a mud-caked palm, tower's bell rusted, dulled tongue,
a girl asleep on a rotting throne.
                              A single thread of flax
and the world went dark: a cursed girl, left by a father for dead.
Roses clotted and thorned the gates; even daylight
dimmed wicked there, the pin-sharp shadows growing tall.

Then the man who smelled like a king—
boxwood and exotic citrus—peered in,
his hounds wailing plaintive,
quivering legs commanded to stay.
The sight of her lying there, unnatural sleep
an elixir paling her cheeks, brought him in.
He trembled, her beauty
                              still and silent
as a copse of willow, as a cool corpse on the field.
He cops a feel. His luck: the sleeping can't scream.
She wants to warn the girl in the story
how she'll really wake: alone again, all in ruin

around her, still cursed to see the hatchet
of the coming dawn strike through the dark.
Since no one saw, it is forgotten: her trellised veins
cloyed to bruise, the moths startling from her dress
like a hundred prayers sent up.

Daughter as Pallid Bat in the Attic

One twilight it happened: Crawling into the house
through a crack, you circled the attic, past mounds
of outgrown clothes, silent wind chimes,
a dollhouse dusted the color of mud.

In the weak, slatted daylight, you fold yourself
in thick curtains, each night the same throwing down
of inaudible call for moth or cricket. You do what you must:
beam to beam and back, surveying the breadth
of the trap, you find a thing to feed on in the dark.

Daughter as Pig in the House

I have winnowed it down to a stalk,
my sin: all the ways I give in, the ways

I make a dim picture, afternoons cooling
in mud under the sky, white scrim.

The roses droop hot and dumb.
I recast my sin as a house of twigs:

branches the color of paraffin, grasses
slicing distant towns to shreds.

The evenings flood color:
a yellowed lamp, a tongue red.

He threats the door open: *listen*
oh listen and I make my sin a double:

inside, the mirror shows
some sow-cheeked girl.

Behind her, his angled jaw, thick hair,
gray-toothed grin: *I'll blow your house in.*

Letter to my father as Severed Goat Head

wrecked today by its lack of lesson—

without twitch and flick, the fine whiskers
mourn the nose's unmoving. Like a specimen,

repulsed as I cradle it

thin glass eye

the sharpest blade. My hate for this house
rings a vesper. I gather the stain and hair like

swish of tendons, the gallop, and the strike.

Letter to my father as month of august

                                                        white sky

      summer is broken by swallows

and the morning flocks,

          a soaked dress hung on a body

In this bird hour

        women keen a jagged grief.

      heaps braided garlands

      still warm   The goats in their arms

        spilling open

What to Wear to a father's funeral

A chain around your neck of fingernail moons
to rend and scatter about the grave.
Regrets like stitches along your hem.
A little tin bird slipped into your pocket.
As a sash, the river where he washed
your clothes, the silt of its dark bed. In your hair,
the frozen bat he stepped on one winter night.
The pop of bacon grease smudged
around your eyes. The rough firewood
that you helped chop, the spark and smoke.
A hat stuffed with his whispered prayers in the dark,
and two handfuls of sand to throw on top.
As a brooch, the O of your keening mother's mouth.
Anger as a handkerchief at your waist—
tucked in deep, so that only the smallest corner shows.

Letter to my father as Robin in the field

small, nervous heart that failed?

No—

rust-colored ruff blooms blood.

at him the grackles pick, their

black glistening beaks

feathers cast off

the slim shining cords

Home

Sometimes when I walk the path next to the field
when I see my footprints walk in the mud behind me like a second person

when the red flock of pine needles weighs down the shed roof
when the irises have pushed past flower to thick, pale pod

I think of our first autumn in this house:
how the birds collected at the feeder like supplicants

at the altar of our great fortune, being *here* and *alive*—
but I never thought about that then, knew nothing

of the way the next year would feed us loss with the first frost,
the way those we loved would later hurt,

of who'd be left to pack up what remained,
of who would leave us in the waste and blank of his death

Sometimes I can see us sitting in the past field's flush and daze
Sometimes we pull him back from the river gasping

fairgrounds

You ask why I now remember:
my hand small in his as we walked at the fair,
stopping to pet the penned goat
and choose a caramel apple from the booth.
Dust flew up in gasps
along the fairground's curving road
as my mother watched me cling to him
through the crowds in the dry afternoon,
as we left her by the broken carousel.

Because today she asked me how
I could have ever wanted to hold his hand,
how I ever picked him to spend a morning with,
sloshing water from a pink plastic pail
onto the dead geraniums in the yard.
She asked as if she didn't choose him daily,
as if a snake were never a beautiful thing
sleeping coiled, and she never wanted
the brief slick gleam of sun on its skin
to be all that there was, never wanted
its fixed stare to be one of love.

fatHER as DistaNt Boat

Far across the lake, on the other shore, the family takes off their hats,
loosens their neckties, unbraids their hair. There is a man and woman,
a girl and small dog with soft ears. They board you
through the mist and stink of weeds. You pitch wildly.

Not until the shore's too far gone will they realize
the wood underfoot is rotten soft. Delicately,
like a slowly flooding room, it will dawn
on them: no one ever survives you. At sunset
they'll leap from your edges like flames.

fᴀᴛʜᴇʀ as Sᴜɪᴛ of ᴀʀᴍᴏʀ

I imagine you, too, began as hide, leather and bone,
matured to smooth-coiled mail, the articulation of steel.
Gorget, pauldrons, gauntlets and greaves, you adapted
to the weaponry used against you—the insult's blunt arrow,
mace of a well-placed fist. You saw the distant flags
and standards, heard the blood-warm steady drum.
And finally, one day your visor slammed shut.

In the Marriage Season

I never walked the front lawn, dandelions and wild daisies in hand,
pretending to be wed; my stuffed rabbits and geese were never attendants
to that sort of union.—But this morning the dove cried its low dark call,
and I couldn't help but notice when another cast its shadow wild on the yard,
tearing toward the first with the whole weight of its life.

Letter to my father as theropod exhibit

suspended in the gallery

absent the skin,

the illustrative terror.

fluttering

strung-up

hollow bones

Letter to my father in the Blue Hour

              like paper hearts pinned to a tree.

That tree was me.

                    return to the cracked-glass sand

      in dresses stark as tundra swans,

               the crushed fronds.

      fish-pale moon

                    an evening storm—

quick, and out of so much dead calm.

Notes

Many of the fairy-tale-based poems in this collection were inspired by the *Pentamerone* by the seventeenth-century poet Giambattista Basile.

"Something He'd Do" borrows (or, slightly amends) its title and owes its genesis to Frannie Lindsay's poem "Something He Did."

"In the Sick Room" borrows its structure and movement from Karyna McGlynn's "Bluff."

"The Gown" and "Daughter as Sister in Many Layers" owe considerable debt to Brian Teare's collection *The Room Where I Was Born*. All of the poems here were, in some way, encouraged in revision by the fact of his book and the considerable beauty (and genius) therein.

"In the Marriage Season" was influenced by Christine Garren's *Among the Monarchs*.

Wisconsin Poetry Series

Ronald Wallace, *Series Editor*

New Jersey (B) • Betsy Andrews

Salt (B) • Renée Ashley

Horizon Note (B) • Robin Behn

About Crows (FP) • Craig Blais

Mrs. Dumpty (FP) • Chana Bloch

The Declarable Future (4L) • Jennifer Boyden

The Mouths of Grazing Things (B) • Jennifer Boyden

Help Is on the Way (4L) • John Brehm

Sea of Faith (B) • John Brehm

Reunion (FP) • Fleda Brown

Brief Landing on the Earth's Surface (B) • Juanita Brunk

Ejo: Poems, Rwanda, 1991–1994 (FP) • Derick Burleson

Jagged with Love (B) • Susanna Childress

Almost Nothing to Be Scared Of (4L) • David Clewell

Now We're Getting Somewhere (FP) • David Clewell

Taken Somehow by Surprise (4L) • David Clewell

Borrowed Dress (FP) • Cathy Colman

Places/Everyone (B) • Jim Daniels

Darkroom (B) • Jazzy Danziger

And Her Soul Out of Nothing (B) • Olena Kalytiak Davis

My Favorite Tyrants (B) • Joanne Diaz

Talking to Strangers (B) • Patricia Dobler

Immortality (4L) • Alan Feldman

A Sail to Great Island (FP) • Alan Feldman

A Field Guide to the Heavens (B) • Frank X. Gaspar

The Royal Baker's Daughter (FP) • Barbara Goldberg

Funny (FP) • Jennifer Michael Hecht

(B) = Winner of the Brittingham Prize in Poetry

(FP) = Winner of the Felix Pollak Prize in Poetry

(4L) = Winner of the Four Lakes Prize in Poetry